Joseph of Nazareth

Icon of the Father's Love

Dennis J. Billy, C.Ss.R.

En Route Books and Media, LLC
Saint Louis, MO

Make the time

En Route Books and Media, LLC
5705 Rhodes Avenue
St. Louis, MO 63109

Contact us at
contactus@enroutebooksandmedia.com

Cover Credit: Nazareth, Israel. Hall in the dungeon under the St. Joseph's Church wall in the old city of Nazareth in Israel, Mosaic depicting the Holy Family, Photo 193986570 © Ryszard Parys | Dreamstime.com

Copyright 2024 Dennis J. Billy, C.Ss.R.

ISBN-13: 979-8-88870-212-3
Library of Congress Control Number: 2024942780

All rights reserved. No part of this book may be reproduced, stored in a retrieval system, or transmitted in any form, or by any means, electronic, mechanical, photocopying, or otherwise, without the prior written permission of the author.

In honor of Joseph,
Husband of Mary,
Foster father of Jesus,
Head of the Holy Family
Patron saint of the Universal Church

Joseph, of royal blood, united by marriage to the greatest and holiest of women, reputed the father of the Son of God, passed his life in labor, and won by the toil of the artisan the needful support of his family.

Pope Leo XIII

Table of Contents

Introduction 1

Chapter One: A Quiet Man 5
    The Ways of Silence 6
    The Depths of Silence 9
    The Language of Silence 12
    The Language of St. Joseph 15
    Conclusion 20

Chapter Two: A Just Man 25
    In the Scriptures 26
    In All Things 29
    In Mind and Heart 33
    In Life and Death 37
    Conclusion 40

Chapter Three: A Working Man 45
    In His Image 46
    A Spirituality of Work 50
    Joseph, the Worker 55
    Conclusion 60

Chapter Four: A Dreamer 65
    The Role of Dreams in Scripture 66
    The Interpretation of Dreams 69
    Joseph, the Dreamer 73
    Conclusion 80

Chapter Five: Icon of the Father's Love 83
    Husband of Mary 83
    Father of Jesus 86
    Patron of the Universal Church 90
    Icon of the Father's Love 94
    Conclusion 97

Conclusion 101

Introduction

Joseph of Nazareth, the husband of Mary and foster father of Jesus, was a quiet man, a just man, a working man, and a dreamer. He was also (and is) an icon of the Father's love. This book is about this humble, courageous man who played a pivotal role in the story of our redemption and about whom the Gospels say so very little. It is a series of meditations about this obscure member of the house of David who listened to God in the quiet of his heart and the silence of his dreams, following God's will even though according to the Law he had every right to do otherwise. It takes the Scriptures at face value and interprets them as a single, cohesive whole and in light of Catholic tradition. Since there is very little historical information about him, it uses the imagination to fill in some of the gaps in our knowledge of him. It seeks to create a portrait of him that is consistent with the way the Gospels and the tenets of the Catholic faith present him. The goal here is to help us see that he is a living icon of the Father's love.

The book is divided into five chapters, each of which focuses on a particular aspect of Joseph's character. Chapter one, "A Quiet Man," wonders why the Gospels record not a single word coming from his lips. It ponders this silence, seeks to understand it, and interprets it in the light of the silence of God himself. Chapter two, "A Just Man," looks at Joseph's Jewish faith and the actions that flow from it. It sees Joseph as someone who puts his faith into action and who lets his actions speak for themselves. Chapter three, "A Working Man," presents Joseph in the context of his carpenter's trade. It underscores his understanding of the dignity of work and how it reflects God's work of creation. Chapter four, "A Dreamer," shows that Joseph was able to listen to the voice of God in his dreams, interpret them, and carry them out according to God's plan. Chapter five, "Icon of the Father's Love," examines Joseph's role as the husband of Mary, foster father of Jesus, and patron of the Universal Church, and shows how, through these roles, he is an iconic reflection of the Father's love for the Church. Each chapter concludes with some reflection questions under the heading, "Joseph of

Nazareth," and a prayer to Joseph thanking him for his saintly life and asking for his intercession. The book ends with a brief conclusion that summarizes its main points and brings them to a final insight.

The book does not claim to be an exhaustive treatment of Joseph but seeks only to offer a deeper understanding of his role in the mystery of our redemption. The hope is that in reading these meditations the reader will see that Joseph was specifically chosen by God to accompany Jesus and Mary during their hidden life at Nazareth and that, as head of the household of the holy family, he plays an equally important role in the family of believers.

Chapter One

A Quiet Man

Joseph of Nazareth, the husband of Mary and foster father of Jesus, was a quiet man. Although his presence looms large in the infancy narratives of Matthew and Luke, he never utters a word, and we know him mainly through the decisions he makes and the deeds he performs. That is not to say that he never spoke or that he had nothing worth saying. He was a man of few words because he understood the true meaning of words and saw that for them to make sense they had to be heard against a backdrop of silence. "Still waters run deep," the saying goes. Joseph's silence, his quiet strength and peaceful demeanor, provided Jesus and Mary with a tranquil manly presence that they could always fall back on and rely upon. Their hidden lives in Nazareth were intimately tied to his. As head of the holy family, he provided for them, protected them, and guided them. They, in turn, loved, respected, and revered him.

The Ways of Silence

There are many shades of silence. It can be a sign of intimacy, as when two close friends walk side by side saying nothing and simply enjoying each other's presence. It can also display distance, as when a stranger returns a cold stare, or an enemy soldier remains silent during an interrogation. It can signal disapproval, as when one withholds a word of approval for someone's misbehavior. It can convey a lack of patience, as when a person bites his tongue and keeps himself from a situation that did not unfold as planned. It can be a display of focused attention, as when a student listens intently to a mentor or spiritual guide. It can offer evidence that one is at peace with oneself, as when one sits peacefully and prayerfully before an icon, a lighted candle, or the tabernacle. It can be a sign of wonder, as when one marvels quietly at the beauty of creation. It can reveal an attitude of reverence toward the divine, as when one sits in chapel in quiet meditation before the Blessed Sacrament. Silence can be used for good or for ill. Joseph of Nazareth, we can rest assured, used it for good. He was a good man, a faithful, God-fearing man, a holy man.

"Silence," someone once said, "is the language of God." To understand what God is saying at any one time, we need to be able to empty ourselves of the noise and useless chatter that often fills our minds and prevents us from listening to the voice of God speaking to us deep within our hearts. Joseph of Nazareth was one such person. He understood the meaning of silence, as well as its power. He has been called "the shadow of the Father,"[1] because he walked in solitude with the Father. The Father, in turn, cast his divine light upon Joseph's earthly frame and left his shadow wherever he walked. The Father's shadow followed Joseph wherever he went. He was a constant reminder to both Jesus and Mary of the Father's love for them. His silence was a special gift given to him by the Father so that he could understand the Word

---

[1] See Andrew Doze, *Saint Joseph: Shadow of the Father*, trans. Florentine Audett (Staten Island, NY: Alba House, 1992); Jan Dobraczynski, *The Shadow of the Father*, trans. Adam Jacek Morek (CreateSpace: Charleston, SC, 2016).

of God incarnate in the fragile child who had been given to him to raise as his son.

Joseph's solitude, in other words, was itself a gift given to him by God that would help him fulfill his duties to Mary, his wife, and Jesus, his son. His silence was a sign of his intimacy with them and with God. It enabled him to listen with his heart and sense things that he otherwise would have missed. He was a quiet man, a gentle man, a humble man, yet also a brave and courageous man. He was someone whom Jesus and Mary could count on. He loved them as his own, and they loved him as their own in return. Joseph of Nazareth listened to his heart, his dreams, his wife, his son, his kin, and especially his God. His silence in the infancy narratives of Matthew and Luke speaks volumes about the magnitude of his heart and the generosity of his spirit. We owe so much to this quiet carpenter of Nazareth. His role in God's plan for the world's salvation was instrumental in its success. Without him, it would have been so much more difficult to achieve.

Chapter One: A Quiet Man

The Depths of Silence

In addition to its many shades, silence also has different depths and intensities. A blank stare is less intense that one filled with vile and contempt. A friendly stare is not as deep and packed with emotion as the romantic gaze of two people in love. The deepest silence, of course, is the silence of God, the Father. It is infinite in its depth and capacity for love. It is from this silence that he utters his Eternal Word, his Logos, the Mind of the universe. God's silence is one with his Word. His Word is eternally begotten from this silence and eternally one with it. The Word, God's Son, is born from the Father's silence and lives with it in peace and harmony. The bond between Word and the Father's silence is the Spirit, who proceeds from the Father's silence and his Eternal Word. Together, all three—Father, Son, and Spirit—form the Triune God of Love.

God's love is self-diffusive. It freely wishes to go out of itself and share itself with others. Although God always acts as one, the three great actions of God's self-diffusive love are typically associated with one of the Persons in the Holy Trinity. Creation is associated with the Father; Redemption, with the Son; Sanctification, with the Holy Spirit. Each of these divine actions have differing intensities of silence that resemble but ultimately fall far short of the silence hidden in the depths of the Godhead. There is the silence of Eden when Adam and Eve walked in intimate fellowship with God, that of Jesus' death on Golgotha and the silence of the Holy Sepulcher, and that of the quiet sanctifying grace of the Spirit given to us through the sacraments, and especially through the Eucharist. The silence within God's Being spills over with different intensities into his divine actions. Man is the beneficiary of these divine actions. He represents the summit of Creation, the height of the New Creation made possible by Christ's paschal mystery, and the transformed, divinized person whom God intends him to become. "God became human so that humanity might become divine," as St Athanasius reminds us.[2] God created us in his image and likeness so that we could be *capax Dei* ("capable of God") and able to enjoy a deeply intimate and loving relationship with him. Jesus took on our

---

[2] Athanasius of Alexandria, *On the Incarnation*, 54.3.

humanity so that those who believe in him might be able to enter relationship with his divinity and through that relationship enter the eternal silence of the Father. In heaven, we will be involved in what St. Gregory of Nyssa calls the process of *epektasis*, an eternal journey into the mystery of God's infinite and mysterious silence.[3]

Joseph of Nazareth was a holy man, a righteous man, a man at home with himself and his own masculinity. A man of few words, he was not threatened by the silence he experienced in the depths of his heart but saw it as an opportunity to listen to his own heart, the hearts of others, and ultimately the heart of God himself. He understood not only the various shades of silence but also its mysterious depths. Watch him as he works in silence with the tools of his trade, quietly reshaping God's creation around him. See him as he raises his son and teaches him his carpenter's trade and the ways of the Law and the Prophets. Ponder him as he ponders his son growing "in wisdom and age and favor before God and man" (Lk 2:52). Since God's actions flow from God's being,

---

[3] Gregory of Nyssa, *Life of Moses*, 2.239.

we can say that, created in God's image and likeness, man's actions flow from man's being. Joseph of Nazareth's actions epitomize this fundamental truth. "Actions speak louder than words," as the saying goes. He truly is "the shadow of the Father," and his silence is a mysterious reflection of the eternal silence of the Father from which the Eternal Word is spoken and God's only Son begotten.

The Language of Silence

"Nothing is so like God as silence." These words attributed to Meister Eckhart, the early-fourteenth-century Dominican theologian and mystic, emphasize the close relationship between silence and the divine. We have already mentioned that silence is the language of God since it was from silence that the Father utters his Eternal Word. When Jesus, the incarnation of that Word, says that he is one with the Father, he means that he is one with the silence of the Father from which he came. No one can understand the Word apart from the silence of the Father. When we speak of the language of silence, it is important not to separate it from the language of the Eternal

Word and, since the time of Jesus, that of the Word-made-flesh. Human language cannot be understood apart from the silence that makes each word clearly discernible. Without silence, words become mere gibberish, a cacophony of meaningless noise. The same is true of the language of God. Jesus, the Incarnate Word, cannot be understood apart from the Divine Silence from which he came. From this Silence, the Father speaks of his love for humanity and his desire to be in a close, intimate, loving relationship with us. When Jesus tells his disciples that he considers them his friends (Jn 15:15), he is expressing the will of his heavenly Father. He and the Father are one precisely because God's Word cannot be separated from his Silence.

Once a word is spoken, it is heard and internalized. We remember words that carry deep, personal meaning for us. Words must be received by their hearers. If they are not, then there would be no reason for uttering them in the first place. Words are spoken for a purpose. The meaning they carry stems from a desire to be heard and understood. The same is true of the Divine Word begotten in the Father's Silence and made incarnate in the person of Jesus, who spoke in his native Aramaic in simple parables that carried paradoxical messages that captivated his hearer's imaginations. The parables of the Lost Sheep (Lk 15:1-7), the Lost Coin (Lk 15:8-10), and the Lost Son (Lk 15:11-32) are just a few examples of the power of his skill at storytelling. The parables were intensely listened to, remembered, and retold to this very day. Since God is the primary analogue for understanding human language, it follows that his own Word, once uttered and made incarnate, would be remembered by his hearers. Jesus, the Word-made-flesh, the incarnate Word uttered by the Father, is remembered by his followers through the power of his Spirit who vivifies his mystical body of believers, the Church, and who continues his divinizing mission through the ongoing proclamation of his Word and sacraments. God's goal in all this is to have his followers share in his divine nature through the person of his Incarnate Son so that, with the Apostle Paul, they might one day be able to say, "I live, no longer I, but Christ lives in me" (Gal 2:20).

The Father's Silence thus utters his Eternal Word, the Divine Logos, who becomes incarnate in the person of Jesus to redeem and divinize humanity through the power of his Spirit who lives in the hearts of his followers, sanctifies them, and leads them to Jesus and ultimately into the silence of the Father, the source of all love. The language of silence thus reflects God's Triune nature. The Silence of the Father brings about the incarnation of the Divine Logos by the power of the Holy Spirit through whom Mary conceives and bears a son and who shall be called "Emmanuel, which means, 'God is with us'" (Mt 1:23).[4] Joseph of Nazareth, the husband of Mary and shadow of the Father, is the person called by God to raise Jesus to provide, guide, and protect him throughout his hidden life in Nazareth.

The Language of St. Joseph

Joseph of Nazareth was a man of few words. Before he said something, he thought about what he would say and pondered its impact. There was a gravitas in his words, a sign of a truly wise,

---

[4] All Scriptural citations come from *Holy Bible: New Revised Standard Version with Apocrypha* (New York/Oxford: Oxford University Press, 1989).

thoughtful, and gentle man. When he said something, people listened. Joseph's gentle demeanor and thoughtful bearing surely impacted Jesus throughout his life. His understanding of his relationship to the Father was surely influenced by his relationship to his foster father, who taught him to reverence God, obey the Law, respect his parents, and love the poor and marginalized of society. Joseph was a working man, someone who worked with his hands to make a living for his wife and family and to make the world a better place. We can say that he spoke most creatively and articulately through the work of his hands. The language of Joseph was that of the day laborer, a figure who looms large in many of Jesus' parables. Whenever he did speak, we can envision him gesturing with his hands in the same way that he carefully guided his tools to shape the wood according to a set design.

By virtue of his carpenter's trade, Joseph had to be a very physical person. He likely lifted large planks of wood and carefully positioned them in their proper places. He had to take accurate measurements and get his calculations just right for sawing and hammering. To do his work, he needed keen eyes and steady hands. He had to be at home in his own skin and his own masculine identity. One can well imagine that his own body language was shaped, at least in part, by the demands of his artisan's trade. It was gentle yet strong; sensitive yet firm; kind yet purposeful. One can also well imagine that he held the child Jesus with the same firm and steady hands with which he handled the tools of his trade. One can see him bouncing Jesus on his knee and conveying to him the same warmth and confidence that he brought to his carpenter's bench. One can see him putting his arm around his son and hugging him in a way that would let him know that he was deeply loved and held in high regard. Joseph was a man of few words, but the words he said were steeped in wisdom and his actions, both at home with his family and at work in his shop, spoke of his deep love of his wife and son, as well as his devotion to his carpenter's trade.

As head of the holy family's household, Joseph was responsible for providing for his wife and son, protecting them, and guiding them. He took these duties seriously and did his best to make sure that his family was safe, secure, and well provided for.

Although by no means rich, his family was never indigent. Joseph provided for his family, giving them all the necessities of life that would enable them to live in peace and grow in their love for one another, their kin, and their fellow villagers. By carrying out his family responsibilities, he demonstrated what it meant to be a faithful, dutiful husband and father. As the visible head of his family, what the Second Vatican Council referred to as the domestic Church, he carried out his duties as a watchful shepherd cares for his flock. His Mary and Jesus, his beloved wife and son, recognized his voice, manifested it in so many loving and caring ways, and followed him.

In Catholic churches throughout the world, statues of Mary and Joseph have special places in the sanctuary. Mary's is typically on the priest's right as he celebrates Mass facing the people and Joseph is on the left. There is a lot of meaning in their presence in the sanctuary when the priest celebrates the Eucharist before the community *in persona Christi*. Their presence there reminds us of the many meals Jesus shared with his parents, a kind of anticipation of the Eucharist he would celebrate with his disciples at the Last Supper and which he celebrates through the priest to this day. It also reminds us that the memory of Mary and Joseph is never far from Jesus' person and mission. Their statues in the sanctuary, which itself is a symbol of our heavenly destiny in the New Jerusalem, show us that they are constantly whispering in his ear and reminding him of the things they taught him when he was a child, a young boy, an adolescent, and finally a man. If Mary sits at Jesus' right hand in heaven, then Joseph most certainly sits at his left. His language of word and action, of duty and responsibility, of gentleness and loving concern, lies in the background of every Eucharistic celebration. Without Joseph, Jesus would not have become the man he became, just as without his mother, Mary, he would not have become the person whom his Father in heaven had called him to be. Jesus was fully human and fully divine. Joseph's presence in Jesus' life contributed greatly to the person who preached on the shores of the Sea of Galilee and who healed lepers and the paralyzed in the name of his Father in heaven. We should not forget that Joseph of Nazareth, Jesus' foster father, played a significant role in the unfolding of Jesus' missionary life and activity that continued long after his own earthly sojourn had come to an end.

Conclusion

Joseph of Nazareth was a quiet man whom God the Father chose to watch over and care for his incarnate Son and the woman who bore him. For this reason, he had a close, some say even covenantal, relationship with the Father.[5] A man of few words, he spoke mainly through his actions. He provided for, protected, and guided the holy family from worldly dangers. He created an atmosphere that allowed Jesus, his son, to grow-up in a close-knit, loving family and extended family of kinfolk in a small, backwater village of the hill country of southern Galilee. He was a man of his word, someone who kept it and held it sacred.

Joseph's silence in the Gospel narratives serves as a backdrop against which the life of Jesus' redemptive mission unfolds. If Mary's fiat made the Incarnation

---

[5] See Carter Griffin, *Why Celibacy? Reclaiming the Fatherhood of the Priest* (Steubenville, OH: Emmaus Road, 2019), 154-59.

possible, then Joseph's quiet discernment of God's will for him to take her as his wife and raise her son to manhood further advanced God's plan and put it into action. Besides Jesus and his mother, Mary, no one else in all of salvation history was as important for the execution of this divine plan. A member of the house of David whose ancestral home was the Judean village of Bethlehem, Joseph was a humble man of noble stock who loved his God, obeyed the Mosaic Law, and lived an ordinary life of a carpenter. A builder by trade, the most important thing he built in his life was the family atmosphere he created for his wife Mary and his son, Jesus.

Joseph of Nazareth was a saintly man who immersed himself in the silence of work, the silence of family life, and the silence of God. He was a quiet man who made a simple living and served his family, kin, people, and God with the humble bearing of a righteous man. Of his many noble and saintly traits, his silent presence in the lives of Jesus and Mary stands out as the strong and steady backdrop against which their lives would unfold and the destiny of countless millions determined. His quiet, saintly demeanor set the stage for all that followed. Although

Joseph was a strong fatherly figure in Jesus' infancy, childhood, adolescence, and young adulthood, he did not live to see his son become the man he ultimately became. Nor did he witness any of the miraculous feats or listen to any of the challenging yet comforting parables that came from his son's mouth during his public ministry. Joseph, such a vivid presence in his son's hidden life in Nazareth, became a hidden presence during his son's public life in Galilee, Samaria, and Judea. As stated earlier, throughout his life he stood in the shadow the Father. Whenever Jesus mentioned his relationship to his Father in heaven, the memory of this holy man, who fathered him through much of his life, could never have been far from his mind.

Joseph of Nazareth

- What is your attitude toward silence?
- Are your threatened by it?
- Do you try to avoid it?
- Do you embrace it?
- What can Joseph teach you about it?

Prayer to St. Joseph

St. Joseph, please pray for me. Help me to be still so I might listen to the surrounding silence. Help me not to fear the silence but to embrace it, make it my own, and turn it into solitude. Teach me how to rest in the silence so I can hear the still small voice of God whispering within me, understand it, and do what it says.

Chapter Two

A Just Man

Joseph of Nazareth was also a faithful Jew. Matthew describes him as "a righteous man" (Mt 1:19), someone unwilling to expose Mary, his betrothed, to the public disgrace of being with child before marriage. He knew full well that he had had no sexual relations with her and that, because she was betrothed to him, he had every right to disown her and be the first among his kinfolk and townspeople to accuse and humiliate her for conceiving a child out of wedlock. Unwilling to do so, he planned simply "to dismiss her quietly" and was resolved accordingly (Mt 1:19). His gentle, peaceful demeanor, however, enabled him to listen to an angel of the Lord speaking to him in a dream, telling him not to be afraid of taking Mary as his wife, since she had conceived through the power of the Holy Spirit and that her son, who was to be named Jesus, "will save his people from their sins" (Mt 1:20-22). Joseph listened to the angel's words and followed them. He was a man who was not afraid to take the risk of being ridiculed himself for marrying a tainted woman and taking her into his home. Elsewhere in the Gospels, Jesus' adversaries imply that he was born out of wedlock: "We are not illegitimate children; we have one father, God himself" (Jn 8:41). Such a statement implies that Mary's pregnancy before marriage may have been known among her kin and fellow villagers and perhaps even in wider circles. If so, it would have made Joseph's decision to take Mary as his wife not only righteous and merciful, but also heroic and courageous.

In the Scriptures

For the Jews, a just man was someone who kept the Law of Moses and therefore walked the way of righteousness. According to the Book of Proverbs, "the righteous walk in integrity" (Prv 20:7). They keep the commandments and observe the various religious feasts outlined in the Torah. Other Old Testament verses describing the just man include Proverbs 9:9 and 24:16 and Ecclesiastes 7:15 and 7:20. In the Old Testament, Noah and Job are men who are considered upright and just in the eyes of the Lord. Noah is called a righteous man (Gn 6:9), while the Lord refers to Job, saying "There is no one like him on earth, a blameless and upright man who fears God and turns away from evil" (Jb 1:8). Also in the Old Testament, Ruth is known as "a worthy woman" (Ru 3:11) and Esther, a woman of great faith and courage who offered her life for her people (Es 16-17).

The New Testament also lists several men and women who are identified as "righteous" or "just" (the two words are often used interchangeably). Luke says that Zacharias and Elizabeth, the parents of John the Baptist, were both "righteous before God" (Lk 1:6). He also says that the prophet Simeon, who held the child Jesus in his arms when he was presented by his parents at the temple and who saw in the child the fulfillment of God's promise to the people of Israel, was "righteous and devout, looking forward to the consolation of Israel, and the Holy Spirit rested upon him" (Lk 2:25). He also refers to Joseph of Arimathea as "a good and righteous man" (Lk 23:50) and, in the Acts of the Apostles, he calls Cornelius the centurion "an upright and God-fearing man" (Acts 10:22). In the Gospel of Matthew, Jesus says, "Truly I tell you, among those born of women no one has arisen greater than John the Baptist; yet the least in the kingdom of heaven is greater than he" (Mt 11:11).

Joseph of Nazareth holds a revered place in this brief account of righteous men and women in the Old and New Testaments. A righteous man, a just man, he decided to dismiss Mary quietly when he learned she was with child, even though he had every right to shun and humiliate her for conceiving out of wedlock. What is more, his gentle yet manly demeanor enabled him to hear the voice of an angel in a dream which told him not to be afraid to take Mary as his wife, since she had conceived by the power of the Holy Spirit and would give birth to a son who would be called "Emmanuel, God with us" (Mt 1:23). He overcame whatever doubts and fears he may have had and took Mary into his heart and home. As her husband, he provided for her, protected her, and guided her. He put a roof over her head and food and drink on the table. After Jesus was born in Bethlehem, he listened to the voice of an angel in yet another dream which told him to take his wife and newly born son to Egypt to escape the wrath of Herod and the massacre of the Holy Innocents (Mt 2:13-15). He guided them on that treacherous journey to Egypt and led them back to the land of Israel when he learned in another dream that Herod had died, and it was safe to return to his homeland (Mt 2:19-21). When he discovered that Herod's son, Archelaus, ruled Judea in his father's place, he was warned in yet another dream to return to Galilee instead, where he made a home for the holy family. Yes, Joseph was a righteous Jew, a just man, a holy man. He was called by God to accompany Mary and Jesus during their hidden lives in Nazareth. We can be sure that Jesus carried the memory of this just man with him throughout his public life, during his passion and death—and even beyond.

In All Things

What does it mean to be just? What does it mean to be righteous? In its fundamental sense, to be just is to give God, oneself, as well as each and every human and creature in God's creation their due. It implies that we understand where we stand in relationship to others and treat them in the way they deserve to be treated. We see the epitome of the just man in the person of Joseph of Nazareth. He was a righteous man, a just man, someone who put himself at the service of God and others, especially Mary, his wife, and Jesus, his adopted son.

Joseph, above all, was a pious man. Piety is that virtue which renders to God what he deserves by virtue of his being himself, the creator of the universe, the one from whom all things come and are kept in existence from one moment to the next. As an observant Jew, Joseph understood that he was created by God and that he owed God everything. He knew that without God he would simply not exist. Without God, the very world he inhabited simply would not be. The roof above his head, the clothes on his back, his family and friends, his carpenter's shop, everything he owned, would disappear. Joseph understood that God expected him to live his life in humble service to the Lord of Life and the Creator of all that exists. That humble service would manifest itself in two fundamental ways: worshiping God with one's whole heart, mind, soul, and strength, and keeping the Law given to the Moses on Mount Sinai.

Living in Galilee, a long journey from the temple in Jerusalem, Joseph's primary worship of God, whose name no observant Jew would utter, was in his keeping of the Sabbath and attending services in the local synagogue. It was there that he would listen to God's Word being pronounced and interpreted by the elders. It was there where his life would be shaped by the Lord's revelation to Israel, his chosen people. What happened at that weekly worship service flowed into the rest of the day. The sabbath was holy and was meant to be a time given over to God. Created in God's image and likeness, man was meant to imitate God by resting on the seventh day after six days of creative work. Just as God rested on the seventh day after the six days of creation, man was called to render worship to God by doing the same. The sabbath rest, however, was not an end in itself. As Jesus himself would later say, "The sabbath was made for humankind, and not humankind for the sabbath" (Mk 2:27). Joseph's religious observance was also evident in his taking Mary and her newborn son all the way to Jerusalem to present him to God for circumcision at the temple of Jerusalem (Lk 2:22-24) and the fact that every year he took his family on the long trip to Jerusalem for the festival of the Passover (Lk 2: 41). Such heartfelt, reverent acts of worship were not ends in themselves. They rendered honor and glory to

God, to be sure, but they also manifested themselves in the simple, humble life that Joseph lived with his family, his kinfolk, and everyone he encountered.

Joseph's piety also manifests itself in his observance of the Law. He tried to keep the 613 laws of the Torah but being a weak human being likely failed in many instances. That was all the more reason for him to take his family to Jerusalem each year for the celebration of the Passover, where the Chosen People of God would remember God's intervention in their lives when he led them out of slavery in Egypt to the freedom of the Promised Land. The Decalogue (Ex 20:2-17; Dt 5:6-21) lies at the heart of the Law given by God to the Israelites, and we can be certain the Joseph took great care in observing them. A simple man, a humble man, one wonders if Jesus' summoning up of the Law and the Prophets in two simple commandments—love of God and love of neighbor (Mk 12:30-31; Mt 22:36-40)—might have been learned on the knee of his foster father, who taught him not only the trade of carpentry but also the importance of keeping the Law and living an upright, virtuous life. Joseph's humility and simplicity permeated the household of the holy family. Mary and Jesus benefited not merely from his faithful and loyal support throughout their hidden lives in Nazareth. After his death, his memory accompanied them as Jesus embarked on his public ministry and as Mary followed him first throughout the hill country of Galilee and later into the Samaria, and Judea, and ultimately to Jerusalem itself, the place where he would undergo his final trial for the glory of the Father.

In Mind and Heart

By rendering worship to God and observing precepts of the Law, Joseph met the requirements of what it meant to be a just man in the Jewish society of his day. These actions, however, did much more than merely give him stature before his fellow Jews. They also had an internal effect, one that touched his mind and heart in such a way that he internalized the requirements of the Law and allowed them to guide his thoughts, feelings, and emotions.

Joseph took these words from the book of Deuteronomy to heart: "Hear, O Israel! The Lord is our God, the Lord alone. You shall love the Lord your God, with all your heart, and with all your soul, and with your whole might. Keep these words I am commanding you today in your heart. Recite them to your children and talk about them when you are at home and when you are away, when you lie down and when you rise. Bind them as a sign on your hand, fix them as an emblem on your forehead, and write them on the doorposts of your house and on your gates" (Dt 6:5-9). Being a righteous Jew, Joseph, along with Mary, likely kept repeating these words to Jesus as he was growing up, so much so that by the time his reached adulthood they were an intimate part of his self-identity. If his Father in heaven affirmed the truth of these words, it was his human parents who taught him the wisdom of these words through the years.

If this first and greatest of the commandments took root in Joseph's mind and heart, the second from the Book of Leviticus could not have been far behind: "…you shall love your neighbor as yourself" (Lv 19:18). Notice that one's love of neighbor is meant to reflect one's love of one's very self. We cannot love others if we are burdened down with self-hatred and a poor self-image. We cannot change the world around us if we ourselves are weighed down by our own self-loathing. More likely than not, we treat others the way we treat ourselves. If we hate ourselves, we will hate those around us. If we love ourselves, we will likely love those around us. Self-love is different from self-centeredness. Self-love recognizes us for who we are and humbly accepts our role in God's providential plan for the world. Joseph believed that he was created in the image and likeness of God. At the same time, unlike Jesus and Mary, the other members of the holy family, his mind and heart, indeed his very being, were wounded as a result of the sin of Adam and Eve, the parents of all humanity. Joseph was a just man, but also someone familiar with sin. The sin of his first parents had an effect on his inner life. His mind was darkened, his will was weakened, his passions and emotions out of sync with each other and outside the gentle reign of reason's rule. Because he cooperated with God's grace and because he lived in such close contact with Jesus and Mary, the two people in all the world who were not burdened by sin of any kind, much of the disorder within his mind and heart, much that was wounded within his soul, was quietly healed, and gently transformed.

Mary's fiat sometimes overshadows Joseph's willingness to cooperate with God's plan for him and his family. We must not forget, however, that Joseph also played an important role in the unfolding of God's redemptive plan for humanity. Without him, Jesus and Mary would have had no one to provide, protect, and guide them through the turbulent years of Jesus' childhood, adolescence, and young adulthood. Joseph was a just man in every sense of the word. He worshiped God and kept the Law. He loved God and neighbor. He knew sin but was not a slave to it. His heart and mind were in tune with his passions. The wounds of his humanity were gradually healed and even transformed. He knew how to listen with both his mind and his heart. He was as whole a man as a man could be. He was the one, chosen by God from among the Chosen People, to accompany Mary and her son during their hidden and very ordinary life at Nazareth, which prepared them both for the challenges and sufferings ahead.

Chapter Two: A Just Man

In Life and Death

Joseph was a just man in both life and death. He lived his life in quiet. A man of few words, his actions spoke loudly across the canvas of history and across the corridors of time. An artisan by trade, he built things with his hands that would be put to use for a time but eventually perish and decay through the passage of time. His family life was another matter. The life he lived with Mary and Jesus was something that came not from his hands (important as they were), but from his heart. He was a man of faith, a man of hope, and a man of love. He was the head of the household of the holy family. Mary and Jesus listened to him and followed his lead. He created an atmosphere of love that allowed the child Jesus and his mother to flourish. He lived his life in the presence of the Word-made-flesh and the woman who gave birth to him. It took a humble man of great strength to persevere in the task set before him by God.

In the eyes of many, that task might seem a very ordinary one. Apart from his decision to take Mary as his wife and the heroic actions surrounding Jesus' birth (especially the role he played in taking his wife and newborn son to Egypt to escape Herod's slaughter of the holy innocents), Joseph lived most of his life in obscurity. Nazareth was a small, backwater town in the Galilean hill country. "Can anything good come out of Nazareth" (Jn 1:46). These words spoken by Nathaniel in John's Gospel reflect the sentiments held by many in Jesus' day. Try to imagine a typical day in Joseph's life. He probably rose early in the morning, before the break of day, to make sure everything was in order for his family as he worked. His carpenter's shop was likely attached to his house and possibly was a room that opened out to the street so he could display the work of his hands and do business with passersby who needed the help of his trade in mending and building the things they needed for their homes. Imagine Jesus as a child watching his father hard at work. Imagine him also as a young boy eager to learn his father's trade and then as a young man who apprenticed with his father and helped him build things so that others might live more comfortably in their homes, protected from the elements, with roofs over their heads, beds to sleep on, and furniture to use. Picture Joseph with Mary and Jesus enjoying a meal in each other's company at the end of a long, tiring day, refreshing themselves with bread, wine, and other foods, but especially with each other's company, retelling the events of the day, listening to one another, and creating memories, and simply being present to one another. Joseph was not just a man; he was a just man. His life with his family was a steady witness of courage, love, perseverance, work—all done in quiet obscurity, the way of so many other members of the human family.

Joseph was a just man not only in life but also in death. We do not know when he died or even how he died. The fact that he does not appear at all during Jesus' public ministry indicates that he passed sometime during Jesus' hidden years at Nazareth. He died as he lived: in obscurity, as so many others down through the ages. The only mark he left behind was his love for his family and friends. We don't know if he suffered through a long illness, or if he died by some accident at work or in town, or if his death came suddenly, in an instant, taking everyone by surprise. In whatever way he died, he took with him what he also left behind—the love for his wife and son, for whom he cared with all his heart. His love for them was surpassed only by his love for God. Joseph, the carpenter of Nazareth, lived and died in the shadow of the Father. He adopted Jesus as his son and loved him as his own. Because of Jesus, we are the adopted sons and daughters of the Father, who loves us as his own. If Jesus is the Word-made flesh, and Mary conceived him by the power of the Holy Spirit, then Joseph enjoyed a close covenantal bond with the Father. When Jesus said that he and the Father were one (Jn 10:30), he was certainly speaking about his Father in heaven. It is hard not to think, however, that, when he said those words, the memory of Joseph of Nazareth, his foster father on earth, was not far from his mind.

Conclusion

Joseph of Nazareth represents the culmination of a long line of figures in both the Old and New Testaments who stand for what it means to be just and righteous before God. A member of the house of David, a lineage which had its share of both good and bad, righteous, and fallen, saints and sinners, he represents all that is noble, true, and just in David's ancestry and progeny. Coming from Bethlehem, a name which means, "House of Bread," he fostered the Bread of Life from childhood to manhood and left him with a strong sense of what it meant to be a provider, protector, and guide for those under his care.

Joseph was a just man and a pious man. He rendered to others what was their due. He worshiped God at both the synagogue and temple. He kept the Law and kept before his eyes the great commandments of loving God with one's whole heart, mind, soul, and strength, and of loving one's neighbor as oneself. He treated others as he himself would want to be treated. He did so because he recognized that, like him, they were created in the image and likeness of God and, by virtue of that fact, made them his brothers and sisters, members of his own family. Imagine him, along with Jesus and Mary, welcoming strangers into their home to break bread together and to share stories about their journey in life and their hoped-for destination.

Joseph's righteous actions toward God and others was a product of his own interior life, which itself was deepened and enhanced by those very same actions. Although, unlike Jesus and Mary, he was not without sin, he cooperated with God's grace in such a way that the tendency toward it gradually faded into the background and his love for God and his awareness of his continual presence both before him and within him became the primary (and eventually exclusive) focus of his life. A just man in both life and death, Joseph, the carpenter from Nazareth, will forever be remembered as the man who raised Jesus, the Son of God, from infancy to manhood, and who taught him in his humanness how to walk the ways of righteousness.

Joseph of Nazareth

- What does it mean to be just?
- Does it concern only one's actions?
- Does it have something to do with one's mind and heart?
- Does it have something to do with one's relationship with God?
- What can Joseph teach us about what it means to be just?

Prayer to St. Joseph

St. Joseph, help me to be a man of faith who lives in hope and is transformed by the power of God's love. Pray that my faith may penetrate not only my mind but also my heart and soul. Help me to live out my faith through my actions. Help me to be humble and just before myself, others, and especially before God.

Chapter Three

A Working Man

Joseph of Nazareth was also a working man. He labored by the sweat of his brow to put food on the table and a roof over the heads of his loved ones. Although his family was not rich, it was by no means homeless or indigent. Joseph worked hard to support his wife and son. They relied on him for their livelihood. He, in turn, cared for them not merely out of a sense of responsibility in being the head of the household, but also out of a love for them that sprang from deep within his heart. Joseph's work was first and foremost a work of love. It was an expression of his love for God, his family, and his neighbors. One can picture him helping neighbors (even strangers) in need by using his skills to help them make a better life for their families. A carpenter by trade, Joseph made things with his hands using wood and tools such as hammer, axe, and saw, a knife and square, a ruler for measuring, and a tool for marking. As a craftsman, he needed a keen eye and the ability to draw up and execute plans for his work. He was a skilled laborer, a member of the working class, someone who took pride in his work and who saw it as a way of giving honor and glory to God.

In His Image

As with all human beings, Joseph was created in the image and likeness of God. This means he was like God but not God himself. For him, the distinction between Creator and creature always remained. Joseph, in all humility, understood his place before God, his Creator. "Humility is truth," as the saying goes. Joseph understood the truth about himself, one that encompassed not only his existence before God but also his actions before him. He knew that God, the Creator of all things, was always watching. As a carpenter, Joseph made things out of the material of God's creation. If God created *ex nihilo* ("out of nothing"), then Joseph knew full well that he created *ex aliqua* ("out of something"). He knew that what he created paled in comparison with the work of God's creation. Still, it bore noble fruit and was a fitting addition to the God's handiwork.

Chapter Three: A Working Man

The Book of Genesis gives us two accounts of God's creative activity. The first (Gen 1:1-2:3), comes from the Priestly author (c. 500 BC) and describes God's creating the heavens and the earth in six days out of nothing and then resting on the seventh day. God created light and called the darkness "Night" and the light "Day" (Gn 1:3-5). He then created a dome that separated the waters above from those below and called the dome "Sky" (Gn 1:6-8). Next, he gathered the waters below the sky and created dry land, which he called "Earth," and the gathered waters, "Seas" (Gn 1: 9-10). After that, he called the earth to bring forth every kind of vegetation, plants bearing seed and every kind of tree that bears fruit with seed in it (Gn 1:11-13). Then he separated day from night and created two great lights, the greater one to govern the day and the lesser one to govern the night (Gn 1:14-19). Then he created an abundance of living creatures to inhabit both land and sea, all kinds of living creatures, and winged birds, telling them to fill the earth and to be fruitful and multiply (Gn 1:20-23). Then, on the sixth day of creation, he filled the earth with all kinds of animals, wild beasts, cattle, and creeping things, and finally, at the end of the sixth day, he created man in his own image: "...in the image of God he created them; male and female he created them," giving them dominion over all creation, and making them stewards of all his creation (Gn 1:26-31). When he finished his work of creation, God saw how good it was, and he rested on the seventh day (Gn 2:1-4). The point of this first creation is that humanity represents the summit of God's creation and that he entrusted his creation to our care. The story is a symbolic representation of something deeply rooted in the human psyche: we are created in the image and likeness of God; we represent the summit of God's creation; we are called to care for creation, rule over it, and make it flourish.

The second creation account (Gn 2:4-3:24) comes from the earlier Yahwist tradition (c. 1000 BC) and inverts the order of creation, placing the making of man not at the end of God's creative activity but at the beginning. It reports how God created man out of the clay of the ground and breathed into his nostrils the breath of life so that he could become a living being (Gn 2:7). It focuses specifically on the creation of woman. God saying that it was not good for man to be alone, and that, even after naming each of the creatures, none of them proved to be worthy to be man's close companion (Gn 2:18-20). To rectify this matter, he put Adam into a deep sleep and formed woman from one of the ribs taken from his side, thus indicating the equal but complementary nature of their relationship (Gn 2:21-25). When seeing the woman, Adam names her Eve and exclaims: "This at last is bone of my bones and flesh of my flesh; This one shall be called 'Woman,' for out of 'Man' this one was taken" (Gn 2:23). The Yahwist account goes on to describe, again in symbolic terms, how sin entered the world. Tempted by the Evil One to eat the fruit of the tree of the knowledge of good and evil, the only tree in all of creation the fruit of which God had forbidden them to eat (Gn 3: 2-6), the woman and her husband did eat of the forbidden fruit thinking that, if they did so, they would become like God and be able to tell the difference between good and evil (Gn 3:5). This lack of humility on their part and their refusal to recognize their creaturely status before God ended in their being forced out of the Garden of Eden to suffer the dire consequences of their sinful action. The woman would experience intensified pangs in her childbearing, and she would no longer be man's equal but his subservient (Gn 3: 16), and the man would toil over the land, work by the sweat of his brow, and return to the dust from which he came (Gn 2:17-19). Banished from Eden, they would no longer be able to partake of the precious fruit of the tree of life (Gn 3:22). Perhaps this was an act of mercy on God's part. If they did eat from the fruit of that tree, they would live forever in their fallen state and not be capable of the redemption in Christ that was to come.

A Spirituality of Work

These two creation accounts complement one another and tell us some important details about what we can call "the spirituality of work." To begin with, work is fundamentally good. Since creation is a work of God's labor, man, created in God's image and likeness, reflects his actions in his own. He is not a Creator in the same sense that God is, but he is in a secondary, instrumental sense. He is, in the words of J. R. R. Tolkien, a "sub-creator," someone who imitates God by virtue of the fact that he, of all creation, is the only creature made in his image and likeness.

Similarly (and for the same reason), man and woman procreate (literally, "to bring or create forth"), thus imitating in a very human way God's supernatural activity of bringing forth life into the world. In addition to the nobility of work, the creation accounts also reveal that prelapsarian man (man before the Fall) worked without having to work by the sweat of his brow against a harsh cursed ground, one that would produce its yield only after great toil and labor. Finally, we find that after the Fall, work was no longer viewed as a noble and honored way of giving glory to God, but as a tedious and painful endeavor due, in part, because man had lost the friendship of God and his reason, will, and passions were now turned in on themselves in self-centered pride rather than in God-centered humility.

An authentic spirituality of work, however, must not stop with the accounts of creation listed above. As stated earlier, although God always acts as one, each of the three great actions of God—creation, redemption, and sanctification—are typically associated with one of the Persons of the Blessed Trinity. Creation is usually associated with the Father; redemption, with the Son; sanctification, with the Holy

Spirit. That is to say that, along with the Father, both the Son and the Spirit are also present in the act of creation. Similarly, along with the Son, the Father and the Spirit are there in the act of redemption. And, finally, along with the Spirit, both the Father and the Son are at work in the act of sanctification. When seen in this light, we can speak of God's work of creation, his work of redemption, and his work of sanctification. The spirituality of work, in other words, has a basic Trinitarian dimension that should not be overlooked. Humanity's fall from grace after the work of creation must also be viewed in the light of God's plan to redeem man through the mystery of the Incarnation and ultimately to sanctify (even divinize) him through the power of the Holy Spirit. "God became human," as we have already seen, "so that humanity might become divine." Jesus entered the world to bring about a new creation. His redemptive suffering on the cross initiated this new creation and is seen in his resurrection from the dead, ascension into heaven, and the pouring out of his Spirit among the body of believers.

If that is not enough, the Eucharist itself represents in a very special way the sacrament of the new creation. Notice how at the Offertory of the Mass, the priest lifts up the bread to God saying, "Blessed are you Lord God of all creation, for through your goodness we have received the bread we offer you: fruit of the earth and *work of human hands*, it will become for us the bread of life" (italics mine).[6] Similarly, he raises the chalice filled with wine saying, "Blessed are you, Lord God of all creation, for through your goodness we have received the wine we offer you: fruit of the vine and *work of human hands*, it will become for us our spiritual drink" (italics mine).[7] As a sacrament, the Eucharist is an action of Christ and thus an action of both God and man. Through Christ, we participate in the work of the new creation. The celebration of the Eucharist is thus a theandric action involving both God and man. Because of Christ, it is both God-centered and man-centered. It involves man's worship to God the Father in Christ through the Spirit as seen in the conclusion of the Eucharistic prayer when the priest raises up the consecrated bread and wine and boldly proclaims: "Through him,

---

[6] *The Roman Missal* (Catholic Book Publishing Company, New Jersey, 2011), 381.
[7] Ibid.

and with him, and in him, O God, almighty Father, in the unity of the Holy Spirit, all glory and honor is yours, for ever and ever."[8] And the people respond in loud voices or in song, "Amen!"[9]

There is thus not only a creative dimension of human work, but also a theandric dimension to it involving both God and man, and a sacramental dimension, one that offers up elements of God's creation and shaped by human hands to provide both food for the body and spiritual nourishment for the soul. All these dimensions—the creative, the theandric, and the sacramental—are reflections of an even deeper Trinitarian dimension, involving all three persons of the Blessed Trinity, and must be incorporated into a sound spirituality of work that human beings can embrace in such a way that gives meaning to their work and dignity to their lives. Because of Jesus, we are adopted sons and daughters of God. We must remember that he dignified human work by taking up Joseph's trade. Jesus, the Godman, learned how to be a carpenter by apprenticing

---

[8] Ibid., 501.
[9] Ibid.

under his father who fostered and guided him throughout his early life. This theandric dimension adds an even deeper dimension to our understanding of human work. Jesus, in other works, not only entered our world to redeem us, but also entered our world of work so that we ourselves, as his brothers and sisters, might share in his ongoing redemptive action. In doing so, he reverses the consequences of the Fall and bestows on human work an aspect that had previously been lost in Adam's sin. As a result, human work not only recaptures its prelapsarian dignity but, because of Christ, is now transformed into a work of both divine and human proportions.

Joseph, the Worker

In 1955, Pope Pius XII designated May 1 the Solemnity of St. Joseph, the Worker, as a way of recognizing the dignity of human work and of being a Catholic counterpart to the International Worker's Day (May Day) celebrated on the same day. In large part, it was also designed to be an alternative to the Marxist Communist Party's celebration of the proletariat on a holiday that had no reference to the transcendent or the sacredness of human work. Since St. Joseph is the universal patron of the Catholic Church, it is fitting that he also would be the patron saint of the working man. As we will see, St. Joseph represents the epitome of the spirituality of work outlined in the preceding pages. He is someone workers can look to and pray to for inspiration, hope, and his constant intercession. As a common day laborer, he identifies with the needs of all those who work hard to make a decent living by the sweat of their brow.

Joseph of Nazareth was a worker. He was a carpenter by trade and taught his son to follow in his footsteps. Jesus apprenticed under his father. Never forget: Jesus, the God-man, learned from a man, his father, someone he looked up to, someone who cared for him, someone who loved him. This relationship around their work underscores the theandric relationship of God's relationship to humanity. Jesus not only entered our world, but in a special way he also entered the world of his father through the world of work. Much of Joseph's daily life was involved in his work. Jesus entered the world of his father. He sought to learn not only the way he made things but also the way he treated others. He learned much about life from the example of his father. "Like father, like son," as the saying goes. One even wonders if Jesus' parables have their roots in the stories Joseph himself told him in his youth as they worked together side-by-side. Although he was a silent man who spoke not a word in the written Gospels, one can imagine him telling Jesus stories about life, about his relationships with other people, about his experiences living in the hill country of Galilee, about what it was like living under Roman occupation, about his hope for a Messiah, about his love for his family, about his love for his mother, Mary, and about his love for him. Of course, all of this is mere conjecture, but it is not outside the realm of possibility. Joseph raised his son from infancy to manhood. Perhaps his silence in the Gospel narratives is because he had such a deep impression on his son that he spoke through him. Perhaps he was closer to Jesus in his public life than we normally think.

There is also a Trinitarian dimension to Joseph's work. His work as a carpenter reflects not only the creative work of the Father, in whose shadow he walked, but also the redemptive work of the Son and the sanctifying work of the Spirit. How so? God, we must remember always acts as one, even though each of his three great actions are normally associated with one of the Persons of the Blessed Trinity. Joseph's creative work as a carpenter, his ability to make things, clearly reflects the creative work of the Father. His close relationship with his son, however, especially around his work, shows a mutual love and respect that has great implications for the meaning of human labor. Jesus entered Joseph's world of work. At the same time, through that very action, he invited his father to enter his work of redemption. Jesus participated in Joseph's human labor; he, in turn, invited Joseph to participate in his divine labor, the work of humanity's redemption. As the patron saint of the Universal Church, Joseph also shares in the sanctifying work of the Holy Spirit and bears that title because of the special role he played in the protection and well-being of the holy family. He continues in that role in the protection and well-being of the pilgrim Church of Christ on earth with Mary as her mother. It goes without saying that in this special role as patron of the Universal Church, Joseph has had (and still has) a special role to play in the mystery of our redemption and ongoing sanctification. While it pales in comparison to the roles played by Jesus and his mother, Mary, it is nevertheless significant in that it points to the role we ourselves, tainted as we are, like Joseph, by the effects of original sin, have in the working out of our own salvation.

Finally, Joseph's work also has a sacramental dimension to it. A sacrament is typically referred to as "an outward sign instituted by Christ to give grace." The spirituality of work tells us that human labor is a good that gives glory to God and, in return, is a means of our own sanctification. While we must take care not to make a false god out of the work we do (a danger that faces many in America and throughout Western society and much of the world influenced by it), we are called to face the humble truth that actions flow from being and that one of the best ways that we can give honor and glory to God is by offering up to him the work of our hands. Work, in other words, when it is properly understood as something flowing from our being created in the image and likeness of God, is a means of our own sanctification. Actions have consequences. Human work, when humbly and properly done, flows from the influence of the Holy

Spirit. It represents the bond we share with both Jesus and the Father by virtue of their work of creation and redemption, and now by virtue of the work of sanctification, all of which are intimately related. When seen in this light, Joseph of Nazareth represents the call all human beings have, namely, to offer both themselves and their work to God. Our work, in other words—what we do, the way we look at it, how we go about it—is a concrete, visible sign given us by God to lead us to holiness. Although work is not a sacrament in the strict sense of the word, it is intimately related to the sacraments, especially the Eucharist, where we offer to God the work of our hands and are told at the end of Mass to go forth and glorify the Lord by our lives.

Conclusion

Joseph of Nazareth, the father of Jesus, was a carpenter, a working man who made things with his hands with the tools of his trade. He was a skilled laborer who knew his limitations, what he could and could not do, a humble man who knew that anything he made was insignificant in comparison with the grandeur of the God's creation. He knew his place in the grand scheme of things and humbly accepted it. He worked hard to feed his family and teach his son the ways of the Jewish faith and the rules of his trade. He did not know why he, of all men, was chosen by God to be head of the household of the holy family. He accepted this task with courage, humility, and determination.

Joseph of Nazareth epitomized the spirituality of work in a creative, theandric, and sacramental manner. He understood that his work gave honor and glory to God and that it reflected the Father's creative power. By allowing Jesus to enter his world of work, he himself was able to participate in his son's work of redemption, a sharing that paled in comparison with that of his son and Mary, his wife, but was significant nonetheless and resembled the way we ourselves share in Christ's work of redemption. What is more, Joseph's work flowed from the very core of his being and was a visible sign of his rich inner life that, unlike those of Jesus and Mary, was not without sin, but that allowed the grace of the Triune God to transform his life to the highest level of sanctity imaginable.

Joseph's work was an expression of his love for God, family, and neighbors. When years later a lawyer asked Jesus, "Who is my neighbor?" we may wonder if his response—the parable of the good Samaritan (Lk 10-25-37)—was in some way shaped by the way he saw Joseph treat others, even those he did not know. Joseph, in other words, helped to shape the way his son viewed God, others, and the world around him. He also conveyed to him a deep sense of the dignity of honest work, an attitude that he carried with him throughout his public ministry of teaching and healing and in the work of redemption expressed by his passion, death, and resurrection.

Joseph of Nazareth

- What is your attitude toward work?
- Do you consider it a burden?
- A necessary evil?
- What is your spirituality of work?
- What can Joseph teach us about the nature of work?

Prayer to St. Joseph

St. Joseph, help me to work for the glory of God rather than as a means of my own self-aggrandizement. Help me to view my work as a way of giving thanks to God for all the talents he has given me. Pray that the work I do may be a way spreading the Gospel message and building up God's kingdom.

Chapter Four

A Dreamer

Joseph of Nazareth was also someone who could hear in his dreams angelic messages from God. In Matthew's Gospel, when he discovered that Mary, his betrothed, was with child out of wedlock, he was going to divorce her quietly when in a dream he heard an angel telling him not to be afraid to take Mary as his wife for she had conceived by the power of the Holy Spirit and she was to bear a son who was to be called "Emmanuel, God with us." When he awoke from the dream, he did as the angel of the Lord had directed him, and he received her into his house as his wife. After Jesus' birth in Bethlehem, he had another dream where the angel of the Lord instructed him to escape Herod's jealously, wrath, and thirst for power by taking his wife and newborn son to Egypt. After Herod's death, the angel of the Lord appeared to him in yet another dream telling him that it was safe to return to his homeland. Once again, he followed the angel's instructions and, because of a warning in still another dream, decided not to return to Bethlehem of Judea but settle his family in Nazareth of Galilee instead.

The Role of Dreams in Scripture

Both the Old and New Testaments contain passages that show God revealing himself to his people through prophets and others especially chosen to carry out his will. In the Book of Numbers, the Lord says that he will speak to prophets through visions and dreams, but that Moses has his trust and sees him face-to-face (Num 12:6-8). In the book of Daniel, he says that Daniel had insights into all visions and dreams (Dn 1:17). In Joel, he tells Israel that her old men will dream dreams and her young men see visions (Jl 2:28). In the Acts of the Apostles, Peter repeats the words of the prophet Joel in his discourse on the day of Pentecost (Acts 2:17). From these passages and others, it is clear that God reveals himself to his people in three ways: face-to-face, through visions, and through dreams.

In the Bible, God gives dreams to believers and unbelievers alike. In the Book of Genesis, Abimilech, King of Gerar, wishing to kill Abraham so he

Chapter Four: A Dreamer

can take Sarah into his harem, is told in a dream to leave her alone and return her to Abraham (Gn 20:1-18). Also in Genesis, Jacob when at Bethel dreams of a ladder reaching to the heavens with angels rising and descending from it (Gn 28:10-22). Later in Genesis, Jacob dreams of God telling him to leave his uncle Laban and return to the land of his birth (Gn 31:10-13). Similarly, when Laban goes after Jacob and catches up to him after seven days, God appears to him in a dream and warns him not to threaten Jacob with any harm (Gn 31: 24). Still later in Genesis, Joseph, the son of Jacob, shares with his brothers two of his symbolic dreams, one which told him that he would rise above them in stature, and the other which said that Jacob and his family would bow down to him (Gn 37:1-10). For this reason, his brothers became jealous, plotted his death at one point, and eventually decided to sell him into slavery. Years later, Joseph is imprisoned in Egypt and interprets a dream of the Pharaoh's former cupbearer who was also in prison and tells him that he would be restored to his former position in three days (Gn 40:9-15). Similarly, he interprets the dream of another prisoner, a baker, and tells him that, in three days

Pharaoh will have him beheaded (Gn 40:16-19). He also interprets two dreams of the Pharaoh himself, telling him that Egypt would have seven years of good harvest, followed by seven years of famine (Gn 41:14-32). In the Book of Judges, Gideon storms the camp of the Midianites and overhears two Midianites discussing a dream one of them had of a barley loaf rolling into camp and overturning a tent. One of them interprets the dream saying the Midianites would be delivered into the hands of the Israelites (Jg 7:13-14). In the First Book of Samuel, Samuel is asleep in the temple when he hears a voice from God calling hm. The first two times this happens, he thinks it is his master Eli calling him, but on the third time he recognizes that it is the voice of the Lord, and he responds saying, "Speak, for your servant is listening" (1 Sm 3: 1-18). In the First Book of Kings, God appears to Solomon in a dream telling him he will give him anything he wants. Solomon, in turn, asks not for power, wealth, or a long life, but for an understanding heart (1 Kg 3: 5-15). Later in the Bible, Daniel interprets a dream of king Nebuchadnezzar predicting the downfall of his kingdom (Dn 2:31-49). Still later, in another dream, he predicts the king's imminent downfall unless he repents and atones for his sins (Dn 4:4:7-24). Still later, Daniel himself has a dream of four beasts, representing four kingdoms, which will judged by the Ancient One and which will be replaced by the kingdom of the Son of Man, who will be given dominion over all the earth (Dn 7:1-28). These Biblical passages show that God reveals himself in dreams as a way of interpreting historical events, predicting what is still to come, of conveying specific tasks to specially chosen individuals. It would do well for us to take a deeper look at the interpretation of dreams with respect to their uses and misuses.

The Interpretation of Dreams

Dreams have accompanied humanity throughout its existence, and there have been various interpretations concerning their purpose and meaning. For some, they are mere projections of the human unconscious. Others associate them with the powers of evil. Others ascribe no purpose or meaning to them whatsoever. Still others say they carry messages from God. It is possible that our dreams can come from any one (or any combination) of these understandings of their nature. What *is* important is to be able to discern what kind of dream you have had and how you should interpret it.

The Biblical dreams mentioned above came to believers and unbelievers alike. They came from God to convey a specific message (or messages) to the dreamer. Sometimes, as in the case of the two Midianites, the dream came to one unbeliever and was interpreted by another unbeliever. At other times, as in the case of Joseph's interpretation of the Pharaoh's dream and Daniel's interpretation of king Nebuchadnezzar's dream, the dream was given to an unbeliever and interpreted by a believer. And still other times, as in the case of Jacob's ladder and Daniel's dream of the four beasts and the coming of the Son of Man, the dream and the interpretation was given to the same believer. Dreams could carry messages of prosperity or famine, hope or doom, life or death. Not everyone can interpret dreams; it is usually associated with the prophetic office. The gift of interpretation of dreams is a charismatic gift given by God to build up the community of faith and often (but not always) has to do with events yet to come. It can be given for a single instance or for an ongoing period. Because the ability to interpret dreams also comes from God, it can be taken away as easily as it was given.

To go a bit deeper into the purpose and meaning of dreams, we can say that they contain the same theandric, Trinitarian, and sacramental dimensions as found in the spirituality of work explained in the previous chapter. As far as the theandric dimension is concerned, God's communication with man through dreams is a work of both God and man. Although God causes it, man must be able to receive the divine message and be quiet and empty enough in his heart to recognize the voice of the Lord and correctly hear what he is saying. Most people, for example, have their hearts filled with so many preoccupations and so much noise from the busyness of life that they are not able to tell the difference between when God is speaking to them through their dreams and when he is not.

With respect to the Trinitarian dimension of Biblical dreams, a threefold dynamic takes place in every divinely inspired dream. The dream itself originates in God and is sent to man. This is a foreshadowing of the Incarnation when the Word of God, the Only Begotten Son of God, takes on human flesh and becomes human. The interpretation of the dream, which comes from God and is received by man, represents the bond between the Father and the Son. That bond is the Holy Spirit, who guides all interpretations of dreams in both the Old and New Testaments. The Blessed Trinity, in other words, is operative n all divinely inspired dreams.

Finally, the sacramental dimension of Biblical dreams stems from the notion that every sacrament has both an interior and exterior aspect to it, one which is an outward sign to the world and the other which has an interior relationship to the spiritual health of the soul. Biblical dreams convey this sacramental dimension in that they have an internal and external dimension to them. Although not sacraments in the strictest sense of the word, each is a visible sign of a divine message from God to the world, formed within the dreamer and interpreter of the dream which has an external impact, for good or bad, on the person or persons receiving the message. "The wind blows where it chooses" (Jn 3:8). The same can be said for the Spirit of God. Biblical dreams come to people from many different backgrounds, believers and unbelievers alike. The interpretation of those dreams happened under the inspiration of the Spirit of God and are typically associated (although not always) with a prophetic mission. The point here is that God can chose to speak to his people in a variety of ways: through face-to-face contact, as with Moses; through the revealed Law given to Moses on Mount Sinai; through visions, as with the appearance of the Angel Gabriel to Mary; and, yes, even through dreams. Those received by Joseph in the infancy narrative of Matthew's Gospel represent the culmination of the many dreams sent by God throughout the history of the Jewish people.

Joseph, the Dreamer

The New Testament records four dreams given to Joseph during the years surrounding Jesus' birth and early childhood, all of which are found in the Gospel of Matthew: the dream telling him to take Mary as his wife (Mt 1:18-25), the one telling him to flee to Egypt with his family (Mt 2:13-15), another one telling him it was safe to return to his homeland

(Mt 2:19-20), and yet another one warning him not to return to Bethlehem of Judea (Mt 2:22-23). Each of them reveals something about God's care for Jesus, his Son, and his concern for the welfare of the holy family. Each of them also tells us something about Joseph and his ability to recognize that these particular dreams were of God, to interpret them correctly, and to carry their instructions out despite the difficulties involved.

Joseph's first dream should be viewed against the backdrop of the angel Gabriel's visit to Mary and her subsequent fiat (Lk 1:38). The parallel with Joseph's dream should not be overlooked. Mary has a vision of an angel; Joseph has a dream of an angel with a message from the Lord. Mary is troubled by the angel's words but gives an unqualified willingness to cooperate with the Lord's will; Joseph, too, is troubled that he learns that Mary has conceived out of wedlock but listens to his dream, recognizes that it contains a message from the Lord, puts aside whatever reservations and doubts he may have, and follows the Lord's will by taking Mary as his wife. Both situations require a capacity to listen, discern, and act. Both situations demand courage in the face of

Chapter Four: A Dreamer

public opinion which, in all likelihood, would raise rumors about the circumstances of Mary's pregnancy and the possible shunning (even ridicule) that might follow. Both situations reveal the providential care of the Lord, who enters Mary's life not only in the conception of her Son by the power of the Holy Spirit but also through the love and care of her husband, Joseph, who listened to his dream and took Mary as his wife and into his care.

Joseph's second dream warns him of the jealousy, anger, and wrath that the birth of his son would unleash in the world. Herod the Great felt threatened when he learned from the Magi that there was a newborn king of the Jews. Rather than welcoming this news that was foretold in the Scriptures and written in the stars, he reacted in anger and sought to kill the child by ordering the death of every male infant in Bethlehem under the age of two. In Joseph's dream, the angel of the Lord warns him of the danger and instructs him to take Mary and his newborn son to Egypt to be away from danger. Imagine receiving the news of such imminent danger. Joseph needed to stay calm and suppress any fears he may have had concerning the arduous journey ahead of him. He also had to have a clear mind in order to make the necessary preparations for such a long journey. We do not know if he traveled with his family alone or by caravan. What we do know is that the flight to Egypt was successful and that the family stayed there until it was safe for them to return. The difficulty of the journey likely paled in comparison with the challenges they face once they reached Egypt. Strangers in a foreign land, Joseph and his family had to adapt to a culture very different from their own. We do not know if Joseph knew anyone in that region beforehand (probably not), so he likely had to start from scratch finding work and establishing a net of friendly relationships that would help keep his family safe and protected from danger. Most of all, the dream reveals the deep amount of trust Joseph had in the Lord. He fled the danger in his homeland, faced danger along the journey, and likely faced danger once he arrived at his destination with his family. This second dream tells us that Joseph was a man of great courage, resourcefulness, and trust.

Joseph's third dream has to do with timing and planning. The angel of the Lord tells him that Herod the Great has died and that it is safe to return with his

Chapter Four: A Dreamer 77

family to his homeland. We do not know how long he stayed in Egypt with his family. That period in their lives was even more hidden than their lives in Nazareth. However long they stayed, Joseph and his family once again had to pull up stakes and face the arduous journey home. Despite all the necessary preparations he had to make for the sojourn home, he must have been filled with excitement and great hope that he and his family would finally be able to live their lives with some kind of normalcy. Being of the house of David and the tribe of Judah, he likely intended to settle in Bethlehem, where King David himself was born, a most fitting place for the Messiah, the hope of Israel, to be reared. Imagine the sense of anticipation he had at the prospect of returning to his homeland and living among his fellow kinsmen. He looked forward to the new life ahead for him and his family. The dangers of the journey ahead were worth the future that lay ahead of them. After all, they had done it before. This would be the final time they would place themselves in such danger. As with any journey, Joseph focused on his destination, had the hope of one day arriving there, and intended to make his way there with his family one day at a time, and one step at a time. Joseph's planning, his timing, his faith, his hope, and his love for his family would give him the strength and courage to find his way home.

In Joseph's final dream (at least the last one mentioned in the Gospels), the excitement and anticipation of returning to his homeland in Judea are dampened when he learns that the region was now being ruled by Herod's son, Archelaus, and that returning there would likely put them in danger. Warned in a dream not to return to his ancestral homeland, he settles in a town in the Galilean hill country called Nazareth. If Joseph's second and third dreams are about fleeing danger and returning home, his fourth is about staying safe. Joseph knew that in Nazareth Jesus would grow up out of the limelight. He himself must have lived there for some time since that was where he met Mary, his betrothed and future wife. As we have seen earlier, Nathanial's derogatory reference about nothing good coming from Nazareth (Jn 1: 46) was likely a commonly held opinion about this backwater Galilean town. Joseph knew that Jesus and Mary would be out of sight and therefore out of mind in that small country village. When seen in this light,

Chapter Four: A Dreamer

Jesus' hidden life at Nazareth was providentially planned by God and carefully carried out by Joseph. Because of this dream, Jesus's early life was typical of any first-century Jew in Galilee. Life, for him, was no different from the others in his village, so much so that, when he visited there during his public ministry, they marveled at his wisdom and miraculous powers saying, "Is not this the carpenter's son?" (Mt 13:55; Mk 6:3). They found it hard to believe that a prophet had arisen from among them, in their very midst, so much so that Jesus would say, "Prophets are not without honor except in their own country and in their own house" (Mt 13:57). Indeed, it seems that Jesus' extended family, his relatives, and friends, found it exceedingly difficult to accept him as a prophet, let alone the Messiah for whom they so desperately longed. Many of them even thought he was out of his mind (Mk 3:21). If Jesus' early life in Nazareth was normal and largely without incident, when he returned there during his public ministry to teach in the synagogue and to heal the sick, he was met with the ambivalent feelings ranging from amazement to doubt to outright disbelief. The Gospel of Matthew tells us that he could not work any miracles there because of their lack of faith (Mt 13:58).

Conclusion

Joseph, like Mary, had faith in his son. His quiet demeanor, his ability to discern in his dreams God's will for him and his family, and his courage to carry it out despite the challenges and difficulties it entailed, show that he had been carefully selected by God to provide for, protect, and guide his family during a very delicate and dangerous period of their lives. Joseph was a dreamer who understood what his dreams meant and who acted upon them. Only a saintly man, someone who knew how to listen and discern, who was sensitive to and able to respond to the promptings of the Spirit, could fulfill the task of being head of the household of the holy family.

What is more, all of Joseph's dreams reflect the theandric, Trinitarian, and sacramental dimensions of Biblical dreams cited earlier. Each of them presupposes an interplay between God and man (theandric), a threefold dynamic that originates in God, enters a man's world of dreams as a foreshadowing of the Incarnation and a consequent interpretation guided by the Spirit (Trinitarian). Each of them has an internal character which manifests itself in concrete action that seeks to bring about God's providential plan for humanity (sacramental). Taken together, they tell us that Joseph's dreams were authentic revelations of the God of Israel, whose intervention in the history of human affairs in the person of Jesus through Mary's humble fiat was also affirmed by the messages communicated to Joseph in the dreams themselves.

Joseph was a dreamer who took his dreams seriously. Although not all his dreams contained messages from God, he must have pondered them all and tried to understand them. He is a shining example of someone who took his interior life seriously and wondered what the ramifications were for the world around him. As the patron saint of the universal Church, his example should inspire us to take our own interior lives seriously by pondering our dreams, as well as those of the Church, and by asking God that we, like Joseph of Nazareth, might be open to listening to and following the promptings of the Spirit.

Joseph of Nazareth

- What is your attitude toward dreams?
- Do you listen to them?
- Find meaning in them?
- Discern from where they come?
- Do you find Joseph's attitude towards his dreams inspiring?

Prayer to St. Joseph

St. Joseph, help me to remember my dreams and to discover their meaning. Help me to discern where they come from and what they are trying to tell me about myself and my relationships to God and others. Please pray that I may listen to my dreams, correctly interpret them, and act on them when needed.

Chapter Five

Icon of the Father's Love

Joseph of Nazareth was the husband of Mary and the father of Jesus, the Messiah. God entrusted him to be head of the household of the holy family. He thus plays an important role in understanding what it means to be a husband, a father, and head of a household. Since the family is said to be the domestic Church or the Church in miniature, his role as husband, father, and head of the household should also give us some insights into what it means to be Church. Let us look at each of the roles he played in the life of the holy family and in the life of the Church. Let us examine what makes him a living icon of the Father's love.

Husband of Mary

Mary was betrothed to Joseph but was found to be with child out of wedlock. The Gospels tell us that she conceived by the power of the Holy Spirit, who overshadowed her and impregnated her (Mt 1:18-

19). Her son would be both human and divine, a person with a human mother and a divine father. The mystery of the Incarnation cannot be explained by the laws of nature. It is a mystery of faith which, while not against reason itself, goes beyond it and must be accepted on faith. As we have seen earlier, it tells us that, because he is created in God's image and likeness, man is *capax Dei* ("capable of God"). It also tells us that by virtue of his compassion and omnipotence God is *capax hominis* ("capable of man"). The mystery of the Incarnation, in other words, tells us that when creation went awry through the sin of our first parents, God did not abandon his handiwork but chose to enter the world he created himself and transform it from within. Jesus, the Incarnate Son of God, was the divine means of this internal transformation, the way in which God would bring about a new creation from the old.

From a purely human perspective, Mary's pregnancy out of wedlock raised some serious difficulties. Joseph, to whom she was engaged, had every right to denounce her for her unfaithfulness and expose her to public shame. A just man who obviously loved her, Joseph decided to divorce her quietly rather than

Chapter Five: Icon of the Father's Love

expose her to the penalties for adultery and claims of illegitimacy for the child (Mt 1:19). As we have seen, however, it was through a divinely inspired dream that he learned that Mary was not unfaithful but instead specially chosen by God to bear a son who would be the savior of the world. In this dream he was told by an angel of the Lord not to be afraid to take Mary as his wife because she had conceived the child by the Holy Spirit and that he would free his people from their sins (Mt 1:20-21). Joseph followed the angel's words, married Mary, and took Jesus as his son with all the responsibilities it entailed. Like him, Jesus would be a member of the house and lineage of David, from whom the Scriptures tell us the Messiah would come.

Joseph was a faithful and loving husband to Mary. He took special care of her because of the role she was playing in God's plan for humanity. He provided for her, protected her, and guided her through the months leading up to the birth of their son. He had no relations with her before she gave birth (Mt 1:25) and, according to Church teaching, respected her virginity afterward. He gave up his life for her and their son by dying to his own self-interests and placing their needs before his own. Joseph, the husband of Mary, was a man of honor and a man of his word, someone who strove the follow the Lord's will for him, even when it meant great hardship and sacrifice. He was a husband who was full of faith in God and of love for the woman whom God had given him for his wife. His love for her never waned and only deepened as they raised their son and marveled at the way God was working in their lives.

Father of Jesus

Joseph was Jesus' foster father. When he married Mary, he adopted him and treated him as his own. Although he was not his biological father, he fathered Jesus in every other sense of the word. Carter Griffin speaks about three kinds of fatherhood: biological, natural, and supernatural.[10] The biological father is the person who impregnates a woman with his sperm and gives the coming child his DNA. The natural father is the person who rears and educates the child. This is the foster (or adoptive) father who accom-

---

[10] Griffin, *Why Celibacy?* 15-26.

panies the child through infancy, childhood, adolescence, and manhood. The supernatural father is the person who leads the child into the supernatural by showing him the importance of prayer and the spiritual life and by introducing him or her into the possibility of having a personal relationship with God.

Ideally, a child's biological father should also be the child's natural and supernatural father. As often happens, however, the biological father may be absent in a child's life due to any number of reasons: premature death, divorce, abandonment—to name but a few. In the absence of a biological father, other men may raise the child to adulthood and introduce him or her to the ways of the Lord. Such men take the children they did not sire, adopt them, and treat them as if they were their own flesh and blood. Such was the case for Joseph of Nazareth in his relationship to Jesus. For Joseph, their relationship was clear from the outset. He knew his place and did not overstep his bounds. He knew that Jesus was, at one and the same time, God's Son and his son. Jesus was an only child in a twofold sense: the Only Begotten Son of God and the only son of Mary and Joseph.

Although he was not Jesus' biological father, Joseph was his natural (adoptive) father and his supernatural father as well. The role that he played in his son's life was in no way in conflict with Jesus' relationship with his heavenly Father. Rather, he was an earthly reflection of his Father in heaven. He provided for, protected, guided, and educated his son in the ways a devout Jew would confront the world. He also introduced hm to the teaching of the Law and taught him to reverence his Father in heaven. In a way, Joseph was a living icon of the Father. He was a window that opened to eternity. Jesus could see in Joseph who was his natural and supernatural father, a reflection of his Father in heaven from whom he was eternally generated as his Only Begotten Son. If this was so, then an interesting parallel now arises with the Blessed Virgin Mary. As Mary conceived by the power of the Holy Spirit, so did Joseph serve as an icon of the Father's love. As we have seen in a previous chapter, God always acts as one, although different actions are typically associated with one of the Persons of the Blessed Trinity: Creation, with the Father; Redemption, with the Son; Sanctification, with the Holy Spirit. If the Incarnation is typically seen

Chapter Five: Icon of the Father's Love

primarily as a work of the Holy Spirit, we now see in Joseph a reflection of the Father's presence, and in the child formed in the womb of Mary the actual presence of the Son of God himself. Thus, all Three Persons of the Trinity were at work in the mystery of the Incarnation.

We might add that, since Joseph was not Jesus' biological father, he has a particular relationship to the celibate priesthood and consecrated life. He freely gave up having conjugal relations with Mary out of respect for her unique relationship with God, one that resulted in her conceiving a son by the power of the Holy Spirit. Similarly, as Griffin points out, priests (at least the majority of priests in the Latin rite [married converts from Anglicanism excluded]) give up conjugal relations in order to be supernatural fathers to the people under their care. They forego one of the pleasures of married life to be living icons of the God's love for his children.[11] One has to wonder if the teaching about Jesus' followers being children of God and adopted sons and daughters of God has its roots in Jesus' own experience of

---

[11] Ibid., 154-59.

being adopted by Joseph. As a living icon of the Father's love who adopted Jesus as his only son, he may be reflecting the intentions of our heavenly Father to adopt as his sons and daughters all those who believed in his Son's message of the coming of God's reign.

Patron of the Universal Church

As the husband of Mary and father of Jesus, Joseph was head of the household of the holy family. Since the family is often referred to as the "domestic Church" and the "Church in miniature," it follows that he would also have an important role to play not only in the life of individual families, but also in the Church-at-large, the Universal Church, which includes the Church militant on earth, the souls in purgatory still making their way to God, and the Church triumphant in heaven. He does so primarily through his intercession on our behalf. What he did for the holy family, in other words, he also does for the Universal Church. As he provided for, protected, and guided Jesus and Mary during their journey to Bethlehem, their flight to Egypt, and their hidden life in

Nazareth, so now does he do the same for the Church throughout the world through the power of his intercessory prayer.

Joseph provided for the physical, psychological, intellectual, spiritual, and social needs of his family. He did not simply put a roof over their heads and food on the table but entered fully into the fabric of their lives. He did so by giving his heart to them at home, praying with them, attending synagogue with them, going to the major Jewish feasts with them in Jerusalem, and mediating their lives to the larger world outside. From his vantage point in heaven, he watches over the whole Church by praying that her material, psychological, intellectual, spiritual, and social needs be met. He accompanies the Church all during her earthly pilgrimage and looks after her needs as they arise throughout her sojourn. Since he himself has a special vocation in God's plan for the world's redemption, he prays especially for vocations to the priesthood, married life, and Christian fatherhood. Joseph of Nazareth, the quiet man of the Gospels, to this very day watches over the Church in prayerful silence and dreams of the realization of the Church's deepest hopes and desires. He watches with

Mary at his side and under the watchful gaze of Jesus, his son.

Joseph also protected the holy family during their time together. For as long as he could, he protected his wife and son from danger and harm. He did so not only because it was his responsibility but also because he loved his family and looked upon them, both wife and son, as a precious gift given to him by God. He wanted not merely to preserve this gift but to help it flourish in wisdom and holiness. To this day, from his vantage point in heaven, he does the same for the Universal Church. Through his prayers, he asks the Lord to keep the Church free from sin, schism, heresy, and false doctrine. He prays that the Lord raises up men and women able to probe the truths of the faith and discern those teachings that are sound and in accord with the teachings of the Church from those that are not. Since Jesus listened to Joseph, his father, while he lived, it follows that he would do so as he reigns in glory at the right hand of the Father. Joseph, we can say, has Jesus' ear in a way similar to that of Mary. Remember how the two of them searched for Jesus for three days and found him in the temple in the midst of the teachers, listening to

Chapter Five: Icon of the Father's Love   93

them and asking them questions. When asked why he had done this, he responded, "Why did you search for me? Did you not know I had to be in my Father's house?" (Lk 2:49). They may not have understood at the time, but they do now. Today, they are no longer looking for him, for they know exactly where he is. The case is different, however, for those still on their earthly pilgrimage. After the incident at the temple, we are told that Jesus returned with them to Nazareth "and was obedient to them" (Lk 2:51). This posture of humble listening exists even to this day. Jesus listens to his parents and takes their words to heart.

Joseph also guided the holy family throughout their lives together. He led them to Bethlehem to be enrolled in the census of Caesar Augustus, to Egypt to flee Herod's jealously and wrath, from Egypt to Galilee when they were clear from harm, and throughout their hidden lives in Nazareth. He does the same for the universal Church, although this time he does so not merely by listening to the voice of an angel in his dreams but also by following the promptings of the Holy Spirit. We have already mentioned that nowhere in the Gospels does Joseph utter a single word. It seems strange that he was present at

Jesus' birth in Bethlehem but was not present at the birth of the Church on Pentecost, especially since Mary was in the upper room with the disciples when the Spirit poured itself out up the nascent Church. But he *was* present! As an icon of the Father's love, Joseph has a special relationship with the Holy Spirit. He guides the Church by the power of the Spirit through his prayers and intercession. He looks out for us just as he looked out for the safety of his family. He is a concrete, visible sign of God's benevolent and providential care for the family of believers.

Icon of the Father's Love

Joseph, the husband of Mary, foster (adoptive) father of Jesus, and patron of the Universal Church was (and is) also an icon of the love of the Father. He reflected this love in his many relationships, especially with the ones he shared with Jesus and Mary, who represent the heart of the Church, which is Christ's Mystical Body and has Mary as her mother. An icon is a work of art from the Eastern Christian tradition—both Catholic and Orthodox—which juxtaposes imagery and symbolism in such a way as

Chapter Five: Icon of the Father's Love

to create an effect that the person beholding it is peering into the beyond, into another dimension beyond that of time and space. An icon is a portal, a window between two worlds that allows one to gaze contemplatively into the transcendent world beyond. The person gazing into the icon believes that the persons depicted there are actually gazing back. When they looked at Joseph, Jesus and Mary received small glimpses of their Father in heaven. Similarly, through Joseph, their heavenly Father was able to observe them in a way that was close-up and intimate. Joseph was a portal for Jesus and Mary to remain in close contact with their heavenly Father—and vice versa.

As with all human beings, Joseph was a product of God's handiwork. He was a work of divine art, created in the image and likeness of God. Unlike icons with figures made of wood and paint against a backdrop of gold, he was made of human flesh and the silent backdrop of a living soul. Although all human beings have the potential of being icons of the living God, the reality of sin often tarnishes their souls and makes it difficult for others to see the divine light shining through them. Joseph, on the other hand, was especially chosen by God to accompany the holy family in its early years during their hidden life at Nazareth. Although he was aware of the reality of sin in his life, his closeness to Jesus and Mary had a transforming effect on him. As a result, Joseph's life with them was inwardly transformed and empowered to walk the way of holiness. He received from them much more than he had ever given them. From him, they received glimpses of the Father; from them, he received vivid pictures of what it meant to live in the Spirit and what it meant to live in a close personal relationship with Christ.

Icons contain not only images but also symbols. The juxtaposition of the two creates a tension that at first seems two dimensional and out of place but which in the end opens the beholder up to another dimension. Although Joseph was a man created in the image and likeness of God, he also embodied certain traits that represented and pointed to the very best of manhood. As we have seen several times in this book, he provided for, protected, and guided the holy family through the turbulent times surrounding Jesus' birth and then during Jesus' hidden life at Nazareth. He also embodied the epitome of what it meant to be a faithful and loving husband, as well as a natural and even supernatural father. Unlike an image which tries simply to capture the exterior features of the object in question, a symbol seeks to uncover the interior aspects of reality. The moon, for example, is a symbol of Mary because it reflects the light of the sun just as she, being full of grace, reflects the light of the Holy Spirit to others. Similarly, the earth is a symbol of Joseph, because his desire to create useful goods by the work of his hands from its raw materials points to the creative work of the Father. When seen in this light, the sun, moon, and earth, are symbols of the holy family who themselves point to the Blessed Trinity: Joseph as a living icon of the Father's love; Mary, as one of the Holy Spirit; and Jesus, as one of himself, the Word of God made flesh and glory of the Father. As the patron of the Universal Church, Joseph continues to this day to be a living icon of the Father's love.

Conclusion

Joseph's role in God's providential plan for humanity as the husband of Mary, the father of Jesus, and the patron of the Universal Church gives him a unique place in God's redemptive plan for humanity and places him in the very heart of the Church. As a husband, he loved Mary as if she were bone of his bones and flesh of his flesh (Gn 2:25), even though he never had conjugal relations with her. As a father to Jesus, he treated his adopted his son as if he were his own flesh, even though he was not. As patron of the Universal Church, he seeks to this day through his prayers to provide for, guide, and protect the faithful during their pilgrimage on earth as he did in a more visible, hands-on manner during his time on earth.

Joseph was (and is) a living icon of the Father's love. When we look at him, we get a glimpse at how the Father loves us and how we are called to love him in return. We see in him the Father's desire to help us find our way home and, in Joseph, a glimpse of what it is like to be a member of a holy family. Although there is only one holy family—Jesus, Mary, and Joseph—we are all called to look to them as they look to us and welcome us not only into their home but also into their family. There is only one holy family but it, in turn, is itself an icon of the family of God.

Icons are, first and foremost, meant to be instruments of prayer. We can pray before one using words, either through written prayers or spontaneously from the heart. We can meditate before one by reflecting quietly upon the holy figures it represents. We can simply gaze upon one contemplatively in wordless prayer. As an icon of the Father's love, Joseph is also meant to be an instrument of prayer. We can pray to him vocally through prayers of pious devotion. We can simply talk to him from our hearts. We can meditate upon his courageous life and loving actions. We can quietly ponder the figure who was so important in the life of the holy family and now in the life of the Church. We can bring our needs to him and ask him to bring them to Our Blessed Mother and to the Lord himself. We should pray to Joseph, meditate upon him, contemplate him, and ask him to provide for us on our spiritual journey, guide us step by step, and protect us from the powers of evil that we will surely meet along the way.

Joseph of Nazareth

- What is an icon?
- Of what does it consist?
- What is its primary purpose?

- How does one pray before it?
- In what sense is Joseph an icon of the Father's love?

Prayer to St. Joseph

St. Joseph, help me to draw so close to God that he shines through me and touches the hearts of those around me. Pray that, like you, I may be a living icon of the Father's love. Pray that I may follow the Father's will for me in all things despite whatever challenges arise.

Conclusion

Joseph of Nazareth was a hard-working man of great faith and courage. He loved his family and did everything he could to give them a peaceful and loving home. A carpenter by trade, he built things with his hands and was generous with his time for those in need. He centered his life on God and family and, in doing so, became a saint. The husband of Mary, the foster father of Jesus, the patron of the Universal Church, he played an important role in God's plan for humanity and all the world. A humble and quiet man who listened to his dreams and carried out God's will for him and his family, he never neglected his responsibilities to God, his family, or his fellowman. His relationship to Jesus and Mary was unique in all the world. Although he died before Jesus embarked on his public ministry, his memory likely followed his adopted son throughout the rest of his earthly sojourn—and beyond. How could it not?

Joseph was an icon of the Father's love. When Jesus looked at him, he saw a reflection of his heavenly Father. His love for Joseph was, in turn, a reflection of his love for his Father. His assertion, "The Father and I are one" (Jn 10:30) comes not only from his unique relationship to the God of Israel, whom he addressed as "Abba, Father," but also (at least in part) from the deep respect and intimate relationship he had with the only other father he had ever known, Joseph, the humble carpenter of Nazareth. God the Father, in other words, used Joseph as a way of being present to Jesus throughout his early life. He chose Joseph, a devout and righteous man who revered the God of his fathers and kept the Law, to be a special instrument in his divine plan for humanity. Sanctified by the presence of Jesus and Mary in his own life, Joseph was so transparent in mind and heart that the presence of the Father could shine brightly through him. If Jesus entered our world because of Mary's humble *fiat*, then Jesus left Nazareth to begin his public ministry and eventually journey to Jerusalem, with the memory of Joseph, his father, deeply rooted in his mind and heart.

Joseph of Nazareth was an important figure in the lives of Jesus and Mary and should also be for us. We would do well to pray to him and ask him to provide for us, protect us, and guide us throughout our lives. As head of the household of the holy family and as patron saint of the Universal Church, he is, at this very moment, quietly watching over us with Mary and Jesus near him, praying for us, and interceding for us. Let us give thanks to God for the gift of this brave and humble man. Let us seek to imitate him by receiving Jesus and Mary into our lives and especially into our hearts as he did. Let us give honor and glory to the God he worshiped and let us ask him to do for us what he did for Jesus and Mary. St. Joseph, the carpenter of Nazareth, pray for us!

www.ingramcontent.com/pod-product-compliance
Lightning Source LLC
Chambersburg PA
CBHW060844050426
42453CB00008B/828